MW00650630

Landscape Architect Registration Examination

LARE Review
Section A
Practice Problems

Project and Construction Administration

Second Edition

Matt Mathes, ASLA

Professional Publications, Inc. • Belmont, CA

How to Locate and Report Errata for This Book

At Professional Publications, we do our best to bring you error-free books. But when errors do occur, we want to make sure you can view corrections and report any potential errors you find, so the errors cause as little confusion as possible.

A current list of known errata and other updates for this book is available on the PPI website at **www.ppi2pass.com/errata**. We update the errata page as often as necessary, so check in regularly. You will also find instructions for submitting suspected errata. We are grateful to every reader who takes the time to help us improve the quality of our books by pointing out an error.

**LARE REVIEW, SECTION A PRACTICE PROBLEMS:
PROJECT AND CONSTRUCTION ADMINISTRATION
Second Edition**

Current printing of this edition: 1

Printing History

edition number	printing number	update
1	1	New book.
2	1	New edition.

Copyright © 2007 by Professional Publications, Inc. (PPI) All rights reserved. No part of this publication may be reproduced, stored in a retrieval system, or transmitted, in any form or by any means, electronic, mechanical, photocopying, recording, or otherwise, without the prior written permission of the publisher.

Printed in the United States of America

PPI
1250 Fifth Avenue, Belmont, CA 94002
(650) 593-9119
www.ppi2pass.com

Library of Congress Cataloging-in-Publication Data
Mathes, Matt, 1957-
    LARE review. Section A, Practice problems : project and construction
administration / Matt Mathes. -- 2nd ed.
        p. cm.
Includes bibliographical references.
ISBN-13: 978-1-59126-085-1
ISBN-10: 1-59126-085-X
    1. Landscape architecture--Examinations--Study guides. I. Title. II. Title: Landscape
architect administration examination, Section A, Practice problems.

SB469.6.M38 2007
712.076--dc22
                                                      2006051002

Table of Contents

Preface and Acknowledgments v

Introduction vii

Problems

    Project Administration 1

    Construction Administration 6

    Assessment and Review 13

Solutions

    Project Administration 19

    Construction Administration 26

    Assessment and Review 36

References 43

Preface and Acknowledgments

Now more than ever, an intensive course of study is essential to success on the Landscape Architect Registration Examination (LARE). An examination of LARE trends, conducted over more than 20 years by the Council of Landscape Architectural Registration Boards (CLARB), shows that the landscape architecture profession has grown more technically complex at the entry level.

In 1980, it was not unheard of to pass the landscape architecture exam (then called the Uniform National Examination, or UNE) on the first attempt within weeks of matriculating from an undergraduate program, although the passing rate for first attempts at that time was around 9%. By 1999, the level of difficulty had increased considerably. The typical candidate passing the LARE generally held an advanced degree in landscape architecture, with five or six years of college, and had an average of 2.6 years of landscape architecture office experience. In 2004, the overall passing rate was approximately 50% (including scores for first and later attempts, as well for individual sections taken separately), with over 700 candidates taking various sections of the exam annually at four different times throughout the year.

One way to improve your odds of passing is to practice with exam-like problems. In conjunction with a study program involving instructive review materials and courses, solving practice problems can improve test-taking performance. It promotes familiarity with problem formats, exposes areas where more study is needed, and can increase solving speed when it's time to sit for the actual exam.

The practice problems in this book have been developed from three major sources of information.

- direct experience with LARE candidate questions in exam preparation courses
- real-life examples taken from practice in the private and public sectors
- unrestricted lists of subjects tested on the LARE national examination

The questions in *LARE Review, Section A Practice Problems: Project and Construction Administration* are designed to prepare you for what to expect on the LARE—in terms of both the problem formats and the subjects covered. This second edition has been updated to the exam specifications announced by CLARB in 2006. Most problem concepts came directly from student feedback in an LARE Section A preparation course I have taught since the mid-1990s. Students with diverse backgrounds had basic questions about test-taking approaches and needed study materials on topics they might have missed during their school or work experience. These practice problems attempt to address such needs, covering the primary subjects tested on the LARE (Project Administration; Construction Administration; and Assessment and Review), emerging issues, and facts often overlooked in common knowledge.

Helping with my first book and its second edition were several capable staff members from Professional Publications, Inc. I am thankful for the efforts of editor Heather Kinser, director of editorial Sarah Hubbard, editorial assistant Jenny Lindeburg, and typesetters Miriam Hanes and Amy Schwertman.

I would also like to acknowledge the helpful comments of Nicole Horst, technical reviewer. Nicole added guidance and direction on how to better target questions to the typical candidate's level of knowledge and skill.

Finally, my deepest appreciation goes to my wife Kathy who encouraged me to write this study guide and its second edition.

Matt Mathes, ASLA

PROFESSIONAL PUBLICATIONS, INC.

Introduction

About the LARE and Section A—Project and Construction Administration

Successful completion of the Landscape Architect Registration Examination (LARE) is required for licensure as a landscape architect in the 47 U.S. states, one U.S. territory, and two Canadian provinces that license landscape architects. The LARE is administered by the Council of Landscape Architectural Registration Boards (CLARB). Once licensed in any state, a landscape architect can establish a record with CLARB, which can expedite the reciprocity process when applying for licensure in other states.

The LARE consists of five sections. The three multiple-choice sections (Sections A, B, and D) are administered in computer testing centers across the United States and Canada in January, April, July, and October. The two graphic sections (Sections C and E) are administered in regional testing centers in June and December. PPI's website (**www.ppi2pass.com**) gives information about the availability of LARE exam reference materials covering all these sections.

The Section A exam consists of 70 multiple-choice problems divided into the following subjects. Approximate problem percentages for each subject are given in parentheses.

- project administration (22%)
- construction administration (52%)
- assessment and review (26%)

CLARB provides detailed specifications for each exam section on its website. Since the test varies each time it is administered, the number of problems in each subject can shift slightly. But reviewing the exam specifications gives an overview of the subject matter covered and can guide the examinee's preparation.

Examinees taking the multiple-choice sections will be required to select the single best choice for each problem, within the allotted time for the section. Most problems will present four options; occasionally, a problem will have up to nine options. One hour and 45 minutes are allowed for the 70 problems in Section A, so each problem should average roughly a 1.5 minute solution time.

What to Bring to the Exam

For the multiple-choice sections, examinees should bring two forms of ID—one of which should be a photo ID—with them to the exam site. It is also a good idea to bring bottled water and an unobtrusive snack.

Examinees are not permitted to bring reference materials, calculators, pencils, pens, or paper to the exam. Calculators, pencils, scratch paper, and a copy of the *LARE Reference Manual* (which provides the code requirements and design criteria to be used on the exam) will be provided at the exam site. Any other materials that would need to be referenced, such as wood sizing charts, will be provided.

Successful Exam Preparation

The first step in preparing for the LARE multiple-choice sections is to confirm the application deadlines and prerequisites for submitting an application. Most states have an application submission deadline three to four months prior to the exam date, so examinees should be sure to meet all experience requirements prior to the application due date (not just the exam date). Although not all states require professional experience to sit for the exam, the confidence and skill set needed to pass come from having a few years of professional experience in a diverse landscape architecture practice.

Every examinee should conduct many study sessions in preparation for the exam. Problem-solving speed and confidence come from practice. It is always in the examinee's best interest to observe good work habits and exercise sound time management during study sessions. Examinees should become accustomed to minor distractions during study sessions; the testing centers often provide their own share of distractions and discomforts.

The *LARE Content Guide* and *LARE Reference Manual*, which can be downloaded from the CLARB website, are critical exam-preparation tools. The *LARE Content Guide* gives exam specifications and other indispensable information on exam content. The *LARE Reference Manual* contains specific code requirements and design criteria that might apply to any problem. Examinees should be familiar with all sections of the manual and be able to quickly reference, if not memorize, the critical information from each section.

 An examinee's local chapter of the <u>American Society of Landscape Architects (ASLA)</u> may offer <u>exam preparatory sessions</u>, which present a good opportunity for gaining first-hand insight into the exam and meeting other people who might be interested in forming study groups.

How to Use This Book

This book is organized according to the LARE Section A exam subjects. The percentages of problems presented for each subject approximate those given by the LARE specifications at the time of printing.

To optimize the benefits of this book, readers should first work through all the practice problems, selecting the most-likely answer from among the options presented. When finished, readers can analyze the results by checking the solutions in the back of the book, comparing the given solutions against their own problem-solving approaches and assessing whether their approaches follow the same logic and reach the same conclusions. Based on this analysis, readers can identify personal weak areas and tailor the next phase of study to address those knowledge gaps.

Problem-Solving Strategies

The LARE problems change from year to year. However, the nature and format of the problems will be similar across all exams, and getting familiar with the problem types is an effective way to prepare.

Quantitative problems encountered on the LARE multiple-choice sections will require examinees to determine the correct answers by performing calculations. Nonquantitative problems will fall into two general categories: (1) "basic recall" problems, which require examinees to name, identify, or remember the correct term or concept from a list, and (2) "complex" or "situational" problems, which require examinees to apply a principle, concept, or skill, make a judgment, or otherwise address a complex situation.

To solve a basic recall problem, an examinee should start by reading the problem statement only and should then formulate an answer before looking at any of the given options. This approach promotes better recall and helps avoid confusion caused by seeing similar terms presented in the options. Once the correct answer is deduced, the examinee should read the options and select the corresponding one right away.

Responding successfully to a complex or situational problem requires a specific strategy. Often, these problems will be lengthy and will contain information that requires a recall of basic knowledge. An examinee should read the problem statement and then read all the given options. Next, keeping the range of options in mind, the examinee should seek the correct answer while re-reading the problem and then use a narrowing-down process to select the correct response, eliminating choices that do not appear to resolve the presented problem. Careful reading will help narrow the choices quickly, to reveal or confirm the correct response.

Incorrect answers on the LARE do not count against the total score, so it is in an examinee's best interest to answer every problem. It is possible to flag a problem for later review or to leave one incomplete. Time permitting, the examinee will have an opportunity at the end of the exam to see flagged and incomplete problems and make another attempt at answering them.

A good, time-conserving approach is to work through the entire exam quickly, answering all problems that can be confidently addressed, and flagging the ones that will require more thoughtful analysis. In the remaining time, examinees can go over the unaddressed problems in a second pass, working through the more complex solutions. If any problems are still unanswered near the end of the exam time limit, it is advisable to make a reasonable guess between the two or three most likely options.

Problems

Project Administration

1. Which of the following is a breach of ethics?

    (A) disclosing financial interests in a private project

    (B) respecting confidence requested by a private sector client where information, if disclosed, could be damaging to the client

    (C) inflating the cost estimate of bid documents when the firm's fee is based on a percentage of construction costs

    (D) maintaining a social relationship with a private client while under contract for services to that client

2. What controls the division of land and the land use intensity of development?

    (A) subdivision regulations

    (B) housing codes

    (C) building codes

    (D) environmental regulations

3. Land use intensity is controlled by

    (A) land use compatibility tables

    (B) strength of materials tables

    (C) accessory use limits

    (D) lot coverage limits

4. In a case where unusual lot shape or size prevents a lot from meeting all applicable development standards, what land use review process will allow relaxation of zoning regulations?

    (A) exception

    (B) exemption

    (C) variance

    (D) appeal

5. Which street classification will carry the greatest number of vehicles?

    (A) boulevard

    (B) collector

    (C) arterial

    (D) local

6. Which of the following is a long-life major expenditure by a public agency?

    (A) master plan

    (B) capital improvement program

    (C) specific area plan

    (D) local improvement district

7. What term describes a civil or private wrong or injury involving the violation of an individual's private personal rights, causing injury to a person or to property?

    (A) lien

    (B) negligence

    (C) tort

    (D) impact

8. The terms and times under which certain actions can be brought forward in court is known as

    (A) a statute of limitations

    (B) performance conditions

    (C) prescriptive conditions

    (D) misfeasance

9. A new consultant firm wants to protect its financial assets from potential creditors. What form of business organization should the firm establish?

    (A) sole proprietorship

    (B) trust

    (C) mutual fund

    (D) limited liability company

10. What process is used to resolve a contract dispute outside of the courts?

    (A) disavowal

    (B) malfeasance

    (C) arbitration

    (D) remand

11. What form is used to ensure that a contract obligation or a regulatory requirement will be met?

    (A) financial plan

    (B) financial guarantee

    (C) monetary policy

    (D) money purchase pension plan

12. What form of regulation is used to protect pedestrians at the intersection of a street and driveway?

    (A) line of sight

    (B) sight-line triangle

    (C) best management practices

    (D) active living program

13. Which element is NOT typically required to be in a consultant professional services agreement?

    (A) time limits to perform services

    (B) jurisdiction for dispute resolution

    (C) optional services scope

    (D) basic services scope

14. High sustainability and ecological principles featured in site and building design are ensured by a set of industry standards known as the

    (A) green roofs program

    (B) Leadership in Energy and Environmental Design "silver" certification program

    (C) growth management program

    (D) smart growth program

15. What federal agency employs the largest number of staff landscape architects?

    (A) General Services Administration

    (B) Department of Justice

    (C) territorial governments

    (D) Department of the Interior

16. What process is used to announce the end of a dispute after a hearing in court?

    (A) deposition

    (B) affidavit

    (C) summary judgment

    (D) remand

17. What category of legal claim may be encountered by a landscape architect in private practice for an infringement on creative rights to a design or to data?

    (A) interrogatory

    (B) deposition

    (C) intellectual property

    (D) indemnification

18. Moonlighting is work outside of regular employment. What consequences can result from participation in moonlighting?

    (A) risk avoidance for the worker

    (B) limited liability for the worker, for work performed while moonlighting

    (C) risk protection for the employer

    (D) risk exposure for the employee

19. The American Nursery and Landscape Association

    (A) is a nonprofit organization that publishes plant quality standards

    (B) is a for-profit organization that represents nurseries

    (C) publishes a guide for planting

    (D) provides a method for determining the value of a tree

20. What is the most widely accepted way for an expert witness in court to establish the value of an existing street tree?

    (A) Consult site records of actual tree planting and maintenance costs.

    (B) Estimate probable construction costs, with contingencies.

    (C) Use the Council of Tree and Landscape Appraisers' tree valuation methodology, published by the International Society of Arboriculture.

    (D) Obtain a site analysis from a licensed landscape architect.

21. The term "prevailing wage" in the general conditions of a contract is applicable to

    (A) administrative agency staff

    (B) public projects with federal funding

    (C) landscape architecture firms and staff

    (D) private projects with loan funding

22. A landscape architect has prepared contract documents that specify the use of products sold by that same individual (or firm), without disclosing dual roles. Such action is

    (A) discouraged by state law

    (B) encouraged by state law

    (C) not ethical according to the American Society of Landscape Architects

    (D) ethical if the firm is classified as a design/build

23. A landscape architect adapts an off-the-shelf software program and sells the revised software as a separate product, without disclosing the adaptation to the original software manufacturer. Such action is

    (A) discouraged by the Software Publishers Association

    (B) not legal under copyright laws, and subject to prosecution by the Software Publishers Association and/or the software manufacturer

    (C) not ethical according to the American Society of Landscape Architects

    (D) ethical and legal if the product is represented as shareware

24. A licensed landscape architect has a duty to

    (A) report to the professional regulation board any activity that violates professional regulations, and be truthful about personal qualifications in his or her area of expertise

    (B) design to maximize profits and minimize expenses

    (C) design to maximize positive visual impacts and minimize visual nuisances

    (D) report to the city council regularly on landscape architecture issues, and volunteer

25. Which of the following is a valid reason for a landscape architect's license to be discontinued?

    (A) relocation outside of the United States

    (B) relocation outside of the state that regulates the licensee

    (C) mental or physical disabilities

    (D) unprofitable business for more than three years in a row

26. Which type of gift policy is compatible with licensure requirements?

    (A) Gifts of nominal value, such as hospitality, are allowed.

    (B) Major gifts to prospective clients, to secure future fees, are allowed.

    (C) Major gifts can be provided only to existing clients, to encourage loyalty.

    (D) No gifts are allowed.

27. An owner directs a contractor to intentionally not comply with applicable building code requirements. Which action should the landscape architect take to addresses this situation?

    (A) Enforce liquidated damages clauses against the contractor.

    (B) Make a claim to a commercial general liability policy held by the contractor.

    (C) Report the action to the local building official, in writing, and then terminate the agreement with the owner.

    (D) File an appeal with the Board of Appeals.

28. A major transportation project is proposed to cut through a landscape architect's residential area, and existing trees may need to be removed under the current plan. A hearing is to be held to address tree removal. The landscape architect's testimony will be influential. Additionally, the neighborhood association has contracted the landscape architect's firm for community involvement (facilitating public meetings). At the hearing, the landscape architect has a right to speak

    (A) only about environmental regulations

    (B) as long as personal paid interests are disclosed

    (C) and mention U.S. Constitution First Amendment rights

    (D) and mention American Society of Landscape Architects transportation policy

29. A court action (litigation) has been filed stemming from a professional land surveyor's failure to acknowledge an unrecorded past land ownership decision affecting the layout of a property line. The landscape architect used a survey document to prepare the plan, and a fence was constructed per that plan, yet the fence now exists on the neighbor's property located within a wetland buffer, rather than on the client's site. Which type of law will be used to decide this fence encroachment case?

    (A) case law

    (B) common law

    (C) environmental law

    (D) tort law

30. The need to make price adjustments based on the exact quantities of specified items actually used on a completed project, compared to the plan drawings for the contractor's bid, is addressed by

    (A) consumer price index-adjusted prices

    (B) unit prices

    (C) lump-sum prices

    (D) a force account

31. The term used to describe the Department of Defense's (DoD's) shift toward adopting industry standards for military performance specifications is

- (A) MIL SPEC
- (B) MIL SPEC reform
- (C) DEFCON reference system
- (D) homeland security

Construction Administration

32. Two adjacent states have registration laws regulating the practice of landscape architecture. However, each state has its own law regulating landscape architects: one state features a title act while the other features a practice act. Both states have governor-appointed boards that enforce landscape architecture regulations. The two state boards both have jurisdiction over a landscape architect who is registered in both states. Two separate complaints against the landscape architect were filed with the boards by the same member of the public, and board action was necessary. What type of decision will be made by both boards?

- (A) administrative agency action
- (B) executive action
- (C) legislative license revocation
- (D) judicial authority action

33. A state licensure board has taken action to refuse renewal of a landscape architect's license. What type of legal assistance might the landscape architect seek for representation in front of the state board?

- (A) administrative practice
- (B) trial lawyer
- (C) professional regulation
- (D) malpractice suit

34. A public-sector staff landscape architect has failed to obtain a major public works project bond from a contractor that is required under state law. Disciplinary action is necessary. What charges could the landscape architect face?

- (A) misfeasance
- (B) malfeasance
- (C) negligence
- (D) malpractice

X **35.** What method could be used to preserve a natural open space located at a large site proposed for residential development?

I. capital improvement
II. clustering
III. transfer of development rights
IV. periodic review of the adopted open space plan

 (A) I and II

 (B) I and III

 (C) II and III

 (D) III and IV

36. On a construction site with proposed residential development, impacts to the edge of a wetland can be reduced by

 (A) buffers within upland areas

 (B) restricting air rights

 (C) water monitoring

 (D) establishing right of way

X **37.** What code enforcement action, taken against a property owner, grants jurisdiction to enter a site and remove a site improvement not allowed by code?

 (A) negation

 (B) abatement

 (C) addendum

 (D) assignment

38. What form of fee arrangement most protects a client from high fees charged by a consultant?

 (A) percentage of construction cost

 (B) percentage of prime consultant fee

 (C) cost plus fixed fee

 (D) guaranteed maximum upset, billed hourly

39. Which of the following is NOT a type of financial guarantee used to ensure contract performance?

 (A) assignment of funds

 (B) cash deposit

 (C) surety bond

 (D) assignment with right of survivorship

40. Which of the following is a type of consultant firm that employs landscape architects?

    (A) architectural/engineering/planning

    (B) general contractor

    (C) design/build

    (D) master builder

41. In a design services agreement, what does the term "reasonable skill and care" mean?

    (A) standard care customarily found in the profession, not perfection

    (B) standard specifications

    (C) general conditions

    (D) performance conditions for skill and care

42. What process is used to initiate a claim in court?

    (A) certifying the record

    (B) filing a dispository motion

    (C) filing a deposition

    (D) filing a petition with the clerk

43. The term "short list" refers to a

    (A) document listing a small number of qualified consultants or contractors, used in the process of awarding a contract for a project

    (B) punchlist of electrical tasks to be performed by a contractor

    (C) bidder's abbreviated notes for the computations used to prepare the bid amount at the bidder's office

    (D) method of ensuring equal treatment of all interested bidders

44. The standard way to find qualified consultants is through a

    (A) request for proposals

    (B) request for information

    (C) minority business enterprise

    (D) women-owned business enterprise

45. Who are the parties involved in an agreement for professional services?

    (A) tenant and property owners

    (B) contractor and subcontractor

    (C) consultant and owner

    (D) owner and contractor

46. A landscape architect who is responsible for approving payment requests from the contractor uses a standard certification of payment form. The contract amount at the time of bid award is $2,000,000. Three changes have been approved. The first change adds $50,000; the second change adds $75,000; and the third change deducts

$25,000. The landscape architect has authorized five payments to the contractor, totaling $350,000 and including retainage of 10% according to specifications. The contractor's sixth request for payment is for $150,000. The project is 40% complete, based on measured quantities. What is the total current value of the landscape construction contract?

- (A) $1,750,000
- (B) $2,000,000
- (C) $2,100,000
- (D) $2,150,000

47. A landscape architect faces the most common type of construction litigation from what category of claims?

- (A) technical errors, such as plant quantities shown on drawings conflicting with plant quantities shown on bid forms
- (B) negligence resulting from incorrect design solutions
- (C) miscommunication among the consultant, owner, and contractor
- (D) construction safety

48. What does project documentation most improve?

- (A) prime consultant and subconsultant relations
- (B) consultant, owner, and contractor relations
- (C) general contractor and subcontractor communications
- (D) project profitability

49. In the financial community, what term describes a release of a surety bond for a performance bond?

- (A) expiration
- (B) substantial completion
- (C) final inspection
- (D) exoneration

50. Which of the following is found in the bidder's instructions?

- (A) technical specifications
- (B) time and place to submit the bid
- (C) general conditions
- (D) performance conditions

51. What are supplementary, or special, conditions?

- (A) information about the jobsite
- (B) information about weather conditions
- (C) adjustments to the general conditions
- (D) modifications to the technical specifications

52. What group files the most construction-related lawsuits against design professionals, including landscape architects?

 (A) clients

 (B) general contractors

 (C) third parties

 (D) subconsultants

53. A materials supplier, contractor, or consultant who wants to compel a property owner to pay a construction-related fee should file which type of claim?

 (A) notice of lis pendens

 (B) mechanics lien

 (C) abatement

 (D) request for proposals

54. Which of the following are actually used by judges in decisions on construction-related claims against landscape architects?

 I. standards of practice
 II. public opinion
 III. hearsay
 IV. licenses held
 V. anecdotal statements
 VI. promotional materials by the firm

 (A) I, III, and V

 (B) I, IV, and VI

 (C) II, III, and V

 (D) II, V, and VI

55. In specifications or in an agreement, the best way to control the potential for financial claims against a landscape architect consultant due to an error on the construction plans is through

 (A) a statute of limitations

 (B) indemnification

 (C) statutes of repose

 (D) angles of repose

56. A proven method of controlling condominium project liability claims against landscape architects is to include which of the following construction project clauses in the contract for design services?

    (A) contractor safety advice

    (B) bidding design services on the basis of fees

    (C) certification of payment to the contractor and certification that the design meets all codes

    (D) claim mediation, waiver of client claims, and indemnification from third parties

X **57.** The landscape architect's construction general or technical specifications contain voluntary standards created by federal law. The board that oversees these standards is abbreviated as

    (A) CSI

    (B) CPSC

    (C) AWPA

    (D) AWWA

58. What should be done to address environmental regulations in construction specifications?

    (A) Include all regulations that apply to the contractor's work.

    (B) Exclude the contractor from responsibility for compliance.

    (C) Specify which regulations apply and what will be done to ensure compliance.

    (D) List all known regulations.

59. In the event of conflicting information for private-sector construction contract documents, what is the correct relationship between construction drawings and specifications?

    (A) Specifications are equal to drawings.

    (B) Specifications prevail over drawings.

    (C) Drawings prevail over specifications.

    (D) Drawings and specifications are governed by applicable code.

60. What national body governs the use of construction materials throughout North America?

    (A) Bureau of Weights and Measures

    (B) American Society for Testing and Materials

    (C) National Society of Standards of Materials

    (D) Materials and Methods Association of America

61. Under which type of legal business format could a landscape architect offer both design and construction services?

    (A) limited liability company

    (B) architectural/engineering/planning firm

    (C) design/build firm

    (D) multidisciplinary firm

62. What type of contract document is used for ordering a change by a landscape architect?

    I. modification of contract
    II. change order
    III. stop work order
    IV. partial release
    V. final inspection

    (A) I and II

    (B) I and III

    (C) IV and V

    (D) III, IV, and V

63. What process, included in the contract documents, requires finished project detail in addition to technical specifications and drawings?

    (A) contingency

    (B) furniture, fixtures, and equipment

    (C) shop drawings

    (D) supplementary conditions

64. In the general conditions and technical specifications of a contract, the need to purchase specialized items that cannot be specified in the bid phase can be addressed by a

    I. reimbursement
    II. force account
    III. cash subsidy
    IV. cash deposit
    V. cash allowance

    (A) I and III

    (B) I and IV

    (C) II and V

    (D) IV and V

65. Which types of insurance coverage would NOT be found in the general contractor's insurance requirements?

    (A) explosion, collapse, and underground

    (B) commercial general liability

    (C) errors and omissions

    (D) industrial

66. Which types of general conditions are included in a construction contract to address contractor schedule requirements?

    (A) incentive clauses, and liquidated damages clauses

    (B) commercial general liability clauses, and errors and omissions insurance clauses

    (C) union and non-union provisions

    (D) force majuere clauses, and acts of war or terrorism clauses

67. Which of the following is a landscape architect licensure requirement pertaining to document control of construction documents?

    (A) comply with software licensing regulations

    (B) sign and seal personal work, not the work of others

    (C) coordinate subconsultants' efforts

    (D) register drawings with the Office of Patents, for copyright protection

68. Which of the following is a type of cost estimate that addresses an owner's need to know what a design will cost before bids are accepted?

    (A) probable cost of construction

    (B) guaranteed maximum not to exceed limit

    (C) lump-sum fee estimate

    (D) contingency fee

Assessment and Review

69. A stormwater pipe located on one person's property is actually owned by someone else. Which type of private property restriction would permit such a site improvement?

    (A) easement

    (B) dedicated public right of way

    (C) restrictive covenant

    (D) lien

70. The basic authority of a small city to enact land use plans and zoning has its source in

    (A) police power enabled by the federal constitution

    (B) police power enabled by a state's constitution

    (C) amendments to the federal constitution

    (D) amendments to a state's constitution

71. A chestnut tree is located along a property line of two adjacent properties. The tree was planted by prior owners of both sites. A certified arborist has determined that the tree is hazardous and should be removed to prevent or reduce property damage to one or both homes. The two affected property owners, Jones and Smith, disagree on what to do in response to the arborist's report because the ownership of the tree has not

been determined. Jones wants the hazard tree removed. Smith wants to prune the hazard tree and keep it for wildlife habitat as a snag tree. To resolve the tree dispute, the city planner at the city with jurisdiction over the sites should recommend that the two owners

(A) use common law to first resolve the tree ownership dispute, and then use applicable city code to determine what can be done with the tree

(B) remove the tree to avoid any health, safety, or welfare impacts

(C) prune the tree to applicable city standards for wildlife habitat

(D) consult with their individual homeowner's insurance companies to see if their properties are covered for damage if the tree should fall

72. A landscape architect wants to deliver services for a client's new property located in a state where the landscape architect is not yet registered. How can the landscape architect serve the client for the assignment in the new state?

(A) Obtain a membership with the Council of Landscape Architectural Registration Boards.

(B) Rely upon reciprocity, requesting that the new state recognize the license granted by another state.

(C) Relocate to the new state and then start a project office.

(D) Obtain a membership with the American Society of Landscape Architects.

73. A signed and sealed document that contains the legal description of a property and is required for the transfer of real estate is a

(A) deed of trust

(B) quit claim deed

(C) conveyance survey

(D) survey of record signed and sealed by a professional land surveyor

74. State licensure laws regulating the practice of landscape architecture include both title and practice acts, yet some states with both types of regulations are subject to periodic reviews every few years. What are the periodic reviews normally called?

(A) sunrise law reviews

(B) sunset law reviews

(C) sunshine law reviews

(D) legislative recalls and referendums

75. What do practice acts protect?

(A) property rights of residents

(B) public trust

(C) right of the landscape architect to practice

(D) health, safety, and welfare of the public at large

76. What do title acts seek to protect?

   (A) property rights of state property owners
   (B) public trust doctrine
   (C) right of the landscape architect to a title
   (D) health, safety, and welfare of the public at large

77. The primary function of the Council of Landscape Architectural Registration Boards (CLARB) is to

   (A) provide dispute resolution among landscape architects and clients
   (B) represent state licensing boards, as well as licensed landscape architects, nationally
   (C) provide relocation services for landscape architects who wish to practice in a new state
   (D) provide membership certification for the American Society of Landscape Architects (ASLA)

78. Which of the following is primarily a local government function?

   (A) transfer of development rights
   (B) zoning
   (C) river basin management
   (D) aesthetic design control by a design review board

79. Which of the following is primarily a regional government function, rather than a state or federal government function?

   (A) transfer of development rights
   (B) zoning
   (C) watershed sub-basin management
   (D) aesthetic design control

80. Which of the following is primarily a state function?

   (A) transfer of development rights
   (B) zoning
   (C) coastal zone management
   (D) aesthetic design control

81. The National Pollutant Discharge Elimination System regulations, which seek to control erosion and sedimentation at disturbed construction and industrial sites, were created by the

   (A) Safe Drinking Water Act of 1974
   (B) Marine Protection, Research and Sanctuaries Act of 1972
   (C) Federal Water Pollution Act of 1972 (Clean Water Act)
   (D) Resource Conservation and Recovery Act of 1976

82. The term "floor area ratio" is defined as the ratio of

    (A) the first-floor or ground-level footprint area compared to the total site area

    (B) the area of all floors of all buildings compared to the total site area

    (C) the area of a site not covered by buildings compared to the area of the site covered by buildings

    (D) the number of floors in all buildings compared to the site area

83. Growth management is a state-mandated program in several states, yet the term "growth management" is currently widely applied to other related concepts, such as smart growth management and sustainable growth management. What does the basic term "growth management" mean in the context of existing state regulations?

    (A) a set of state regulations that focus on the rate of change in the size or population of a geographic area rather than the residents' vision for growth of the area

    (B) a set of regional laws that focus on the rate of change in the population and housing of a geographical area rather than the area's environment

    (C) a set of state laws that focus on the rate of change in the population, density, traffic, and housing of a geographic area as they affect the quality of the area's environment

    (D) environmental regulations

84. Environmental regulations at the local or state level that focus on a particular unique region or location by state are usually referred to as

    (A) critical lands

    (B) areas of state critical concern

    (C) critical aquifer protection areas

    (D) critical unique environments

85. A client has a property for a proposed residential subdivision. She would like to set up long-term private rules of use by residents for certain privately constructed commonly owned outdoor structures, located within the common area of the proposed subdivision. The landscape architect preparing designs for the common area structures should advise the client to establish

    (A) a homeowners association

    (B) a limited liability company for subdivision management

    (C) codes, covenants, and restrictions

    (D) a native-growth protection easement

86. The parcel of land located between the front, side, or rear of a property line and the buildable footprint limit area is called

    (A) a set aside

    (B) a buffer

    (C) a setback

    (D) an easement

87. The term "allied professions" refers to the other state-registered professions most similar to the practice of landscape architecture. Specialists in the allied professions include

    (A) sculptors and public artists

    (B) architects, engineers, and land surveyors

    (C) lawyers and accountants

    (D) economists and geologists

88. A street is built by a private contractor to meet applicable city design standards for future dedication as part of a proposed subdivision, which is to be platted in six months. In this situation, what is the proper application of the term "right of way"?

    (A) private access tract dedication

    (B) proposed public right-of-way dedication

    (C) dedicated right of way

    (D) recorded right of way

89. National regulations govern wetlands throughout the United States. Several agencies have an interest in and jurisdiction over wetlands regulation. Which agencies are most heavily involved in wetlands delineation and protection?

I.   Army Corps of Engineers
II. Fish and Wildlife Service
III. National Parks Service
IV. National Oceanic and Atmospheric Administration
V.   Department of the Interior
VI. Office of the Attorney General
VII. Department of Agriculture

    (A) I and II

    (B) I and III

    (C) IV and V

    (D) VI and VII

90. To comply with federal or state law, a landscape architect must

    (A) pay for damages if they involve landscape architecture

    (B) practice landscape architecture in a manner that complies with known applicable federal or state law

    (C) not practice landscape architecture in a manner that violates federal or state law

    (D) comply with the types of laws that are directly applicable to landscape architecture, such as real estate and environmental regulations, not immigration or tax law

Solutions

Project Administration

1. Inflating cost estimates used for fee calculation is a breach of ethics because it places the professional's financial interests ahead of the client's.

Disclosing financial interests would actually correct or avoid an ethical breach. Respecting a confidentiality request from a client is expected in all cases; furthermore, confidentiality is usually a contractual requirement. The problem statement does not indicate that the confidence disclosure is associated with any violation of public regulations—which is the one exception that allows disclosure of confidential client information. Maintaining social relationships with private clients while delivering professional services under contract is generally acceptable, especially in small communities, and option (D) does not specify any ethical concern being at issue in the social relationship with the client.

The answer is (C).

2. Subdivision regulations are used to control the intensity of a proposed development by limiting the site's size, location, proximity to other uses, density, and coverage.

Housing codes is an incorrect choice because the problem statement specifies that the division of land is at issue and gives no information about housing or occupancy. The term "building codes" refers to methods, materials, systems, strengths, minimum standards, and overall quality of development at a site, yet does not specify that land division is at issue. Environmental regulations do not address the division of land.

The answer is (A).

3. Lot coverage limits are used to control size of pavement or building coverage in relation to total site size. The extent of the coverage (10% versus 90%) is considered the land use intensity.

Land use intensity limits a site's location and proximity to other adjacent uses, thus precluding references to land use compatibility tables. Strength of materials tables is an incorrect choice because the problem statement specifies that the land use is at issue, not the building materials. Since the problem statement does not specify information about the relative proportions of the principal or an accessory use, choosing accessory use limits would be an incorrect assumption. Typically, the land use intensity is addressed by zoning codes that might include land use tables or lists of allowable, conditional, and prohibited uses.

The answer is (D).

4. The variance process is used to formally acknowledge and address lot size or shape variation in relation to other similarly designated lots.

Even though, in some communities, exception and exemption may refer to land use review processes that provide relief of numerical standards, similar to a variance process, these terms are both incorrect choices because the size of the lot is not specified in the problem statement. The appeals process is normally used after a land use decision has been made, in contrast to a variance process, which is used prior to the issuance of a decision.

The answer is (C).

5. An arterial street is used to carry the highest number of vehicles, usually at higher rates of speed in relation to other street types.

The terms "collector" and "local" refer to streets having a smaller traffic-volume capacity than an arterial street. A boulevard is normally a street with a landscape space in the center and at the edges. A boulevard might typically be wider than a local street, yet it would not be specifically associated with any particular traffic capacity; it could be a local, collector, or arterial street.

The answer is (C).

6. A capital improvement program is a long-life major expenditure by a public agency. Two or more capital improvement projects would form a program.

The terms "master plan" and "specific area plan" refer to types of planning efforts or documents that might have a capital improvement program as a subset or component. A specific area plan is a particular type of plan, authorized by California state law, that would include a capital improvement program or a capital improvement project. A local improvement district (LID) is normally the result of a component public works project within a capital improvement program. The LID is a defined area or zone with specified properties that benefit from a specific capital improvement project, and it has many local variations, such as the rural improvement district (RID) or utility improvement district (ULID).

The answer is (B).

7. A tort is a civil or private wrong or injury involving the violation of an individual's private personal rights, causing injury to a person or to property.

A lien is a formal written claim against the property record, for the value of work performed or materials provided. Negligence refers to a duty not performed, omitted, or performed incorrectly so as to cause harm to a person or to property. An impact is not automatically a civil or private wrong or an injury involving a violation of private personal rights. The term "impact" is commonly defined as the force or impression of one thing on another. The option does not indicate whether the impact was a cause of injury to a person or to property.

The answer is (C).

8. A statute of limitations is the limit that sets out terms and times under which certain actions can be brought forward in court.

Performance conditions refers to specifications for construction work performance or materials quality. Prescriptive conditions refers to the manner in which an action is performed and is a second type of specification for construction work. Misfeasance is a legal term that means a wrongful act, yet this term is not associated with any particular time frame.

The answer is (A).

9. The limited liability company (LLC) is a form of business organization that can protect a company's assets from creditors.

Neither a trust nor a mutual fund is used by firms to organize for the delivery of consultant professional services. A trust is a financial arrangement organized to protect and transfer assets, usually for favorable taxation purposes. A mutual fund is a type of investment that includes several different securities (stocks, bonds, etc.), regulated and organized to be traded in an active market for the ease of purchase or sale. Although a sole proprietorship is used widely for consultant services, this form of business organization does not protect assets from creditors. A sole proprietorship means a single individual is the business owner.

The answer is (D).

10. Arbitration is the process or action used to resolve contract disputes outside of the court system, usually with the use of a mediator or a neutral party to facilitate talks and record the resolution after it is reached.

A remand is an action ordered to remake a decision that was already made. To disavow means to repudiate, or reject as unathorized. Malfeasance is an improper action by a public official.

The answer is (C).

11. Financial guarantee is the general category of financial forms, typically issued by an entity other than the contractor, that ensures the owner or a municipal agency that the contract obligation for the monetary amount of the work will be met. Financial guarantees are often used to ensure performance of a municipal regulation, such as the installation of temporary erosion-control measures at a site or of sidewalks in a new subdivision. Examples of four commonly available kinds of financial guarantees are surety bonds, cash deposits, assignment of funds, and irrevocable letters of credit.

Monetary policy is a general banking or economic term that refers to an overall policy on the regulation of the flow of capital. Financial plan and money purchase pension plan are both financial terms that refer to a formal document or established mechanism to accumulate assets, or a plan within which to invest assets. They do not refer to the enforcement of obligations or regulatory requirements.

The answer is (B).

12. A sight-line triangle is a setback at a street and driveway intersection that restricts anyone from placing view obstructions at the height of the driver's line of sight, generally located between 3 ft and 6 ft above ground for a specified horizontal distance related to street design speed.

Line of sight is the general term for the vertical view corridor that might normally be 3°, measured up or down, from the height of the viewer's eye. The terms "best management practices" and "active living program" are terms used in documents to refer to pedestrians, yet neither form of regulation directly protects pedestrians at street and driveway intersections.

The answer is (B).

13. The scope of optional services may or may not be covered in a consultant professional services agreement.

Time limits to perform services should always be in an agreement, to limit liability. Jurisdiction, or venue for dispute resolution, should be included in contract documents, to make clear where and how the process of dispute resolution can be performed. Basic services should always be included in an agreement, or in an attachment or exhibit made part of the agreement.

The answer is (C).

14. The Leadership in Energy and Environmental Design (LEED) "silver" certification is a program ranking based on criteria set by a private organization to ensure high sustainability and ecological principles in site and building design.

A green roofs program refers specifically to rooftop gardens. Either a growth management program or a smart growth program might ensure high sustainability and ecological principles in site and building design. Yet growth management is usually a state or local law rather than a set of standards. And smart growth is a collaborative effort in the form of a political action coalition rather than a set of industry standards; it involves both public and private actions rather than industry design standards.

The answer is (B).

15. The Department of the Interior has vast public land ownership as well as several branches, such as the National Park Service and the Bureau of Land Management, that require the skills of landscape architects in various roles, such as project management, design, and planning.

Neither the General Services Administration nor the Department of Justice would routinely use many staff landscape architects. Territorial governments (U.S. Virgin Islands, Guam, Marshall Islands) would have a potential need for landscape architecture staff, yet these agencies are very limited in size and budget compared to the entire Department of the Interior.

The answer is (D).

16. A summary judgment is the only option that is a type of decision or order made by a judge that ends a dispute between the parties in court.

The remaining options are all types of hearing actions. Depositions are routinely used to make statements before or outside of a hearing, when a party cannot attend or when detailed information needs to be recorded. An affidavit is a type of declaratory statement similar to a deposition, except that it is simply a signed written (usually sworn) statement by an individual, not necessarily formally recorded by a court reporter. A remand is an order from a higher body to a lower body for a "do over" decision or action, usually with specific instructions on how to correct or change an earlier decision.

The answer is (C).

17. Intellectual property is the category of legal claim that pertains to copyrights and protection of the ownership of creative works, including the software used by nearly all private-sector professional offices providing landscape architectural services. The remaining options are terms used in the legal profession, yet they do not refer to creative rights ownership.

The answer is (C).

18. The term "moonlighting" refers to professional work done by an individual in addition to his or her principal occupation. Moonlighting can result in risk exposure for the employee or employer.

Risk avoidance is incorrect because moonlighting can increase risk to the worker. Limits of liability can be extended to employers in certain instances, so options (B) and (C) are incorrect.

The answer is (D).

19. The American Nursery and Landscape Association (ANLA) (formerly the American Association of Nurserymen) is a professional organization that publishes a widely used guide called *American Standard for Nursery Stock*.

The answer is (A).

20. The method endorsed by the Council of Tree and Landscape Appraisers is the most widely used system for evaluating the value (based on factors such as location, age, use, condition, and size) of a tree in court, whether the expert witness is a landscape architect, appraiser, or arborist.

The remaining options are reasonable methods to consider, yet are incorrect since the problem statement asks for the method most widely accepted in court, not for the method landscape architects might prefer to provide.

The answer is (C).

21. Public projects with federal funding is correct because federal agency funding triggers the need for prevailing wages in specifications.

None of the remaining options would be included in the general conditions of a contract. Landscape architecture firms and staff may be subject to a state's minimum wage standards, although this would not be referenced in the general conditions.

The answer is (B).

22. Such an action is unethical because the two roles of sales and specification trigger the need for full disclosure.

Landscape architecture firms and staff may be design/build firms, yet a disclosure would still need to be made in the situation described. Response (D) might be a true statement, but the problem statement does not provide information regarding the landscape architect's role in this situation. A firm may be classified as design/build for the purposes of taxation, marketing representation, or trade association membership. The term "design/build" implies that dual roles for design and building (rather than specification and sales) are provided by a single firm. Design/build firms might be discouraged, encouraged, or not addressed by state laws, yet the problem does not provide enough information regarding the ethics of this situation to justify selecting option (A) or (B). State law rarely addresses ethical standards.

The answer is (C).

23. Such an action is illegal and triggers the need for full disclosure and permission, and possibly payment of royalties or licensing fees. Landscape architecture firms may be providing a good service by distributing such software, yet the disclosure would need to be made.

The Software Publishers Association would discourage such action; however, this answer only covers one aspect of the copyright and intellectual property issues. The American Society of Landscape Architects (ASLA) does not prevent the sale of software, and shareware designation does not address intellectual property or copyright aspects.

The answer is (B).

24. Option (A) addresses two duties imposed on a licensed landscape architect—reporting professional violations and truthfully representing personal qualifications.

Options (B) and (C) are typically associated with good professional practice, yet these two answers do not result from licensure duties. Option (D) presents two activities related to good citizenship, yet reporting to the city council and volunteering are not licensure duties.

The answer is (A).

25. Mental or physical disability clauses are commonly found in most state laws, and such clauses enable licensing boards to discontinue licensure.

Relocation does not require a licensee to discontinue practice. Several unprofitable business years might encourage a licensee to discontinue practice, yet profitability is not a requirement that affects licensure.

The answer is (C).

26. Gifts of nominal value, such as hospitality-related gifts, are allowed. Treating an office visitor to coffee, beverages, or snacks at a business-related event would be considered hospitality, rather than a major gift.

Major gifts, given to secure future fees from prospective clients or to encourage loyalty from existing clients, are not allowed.

The answer is (A).

27. Reporting the action and then terminating the agreement may seem a bit extreme, yet this is the prescribed method for handling such a situation. The landscape architect should comply with local codes, as well as inform the local official of his or her awareness of the incident and remove himself or herself from liability.

The problem statement does not give enough information to warrant an assumption that any claims would affect either the schedule (liquidated damages) or casualties covered by insurance. Liquidated damages clauses address the penalty for late completion by the contractor, primarily for schedule control. Commercial general liability coverage can apply to the landscape architect and could also apply to contractors. Filing a claim to the contractor's policy will not directly remedy the owner's action. Filing an appeal is incorrect because the decision was made by the owner, not by the local jurisdiction.

The answer is (C).

28. Ethical public participation where a fee-paid relationship exists is constrained by several interests—the landscape architect's financial role as consultant, constitutional rights, professional association policy, and role as a resident in the neighborhood. Disclosing personal paid interests is the best course of action.

Options (A) and (D) are reasonable actions, but the specific matter at hand does not necessarily pertain to environmental regulations or transportation policy. The problem statement does not provide information on the trees' condition (such as whether or not any hazard trees are in need of removal or worthy of keeping), the landscape architect's affiliation with the ASLA, or the transportation policy (such as whether it is a draft or has already been adopted). U.S. Constitution First Amendment rights would apply to any speaker, and a public hearing would not limit this right; yet option (C) does not sufficiently answer the specifics of this question.

The answer is (B).

29. Common law is a system of laws originally developed in England that result in decisions based on customs and usage rather than codified written law. Court decisions based on common law usually involve equity or specific instances that are not addressed by local codes. The problem statement indicates that the fence is an encroachment, meaning the fence is not properly located on the property where the fence should be located, in this instance because it was unknown that a prior court decision had changed the property line location.

Case law or tort law might be valid answers, yet not enough information is provided to know if either of these areas of law can be used in this case or have already been used. The problem statement does not clearly indicate if the fence was constructed with the adjacent property owner's access permission, so a trespass (a type of tort action) is possible but not established from the given information. Environmental law is not the correct answer because the problem does not provide enough information about the wetland buffer, and fences may typically be found or legally permitted at the outer edges of wetland buffers.

The answer is (B).

30. A unit prices clause allows a contractor to establish a price for an item that can be used for adjustments to the quantity specified in the bid plans. The contractor would calculate the unit price at a specified site area by distributing the fixed and variable costs associated with the installation of one unit over a range of quantities that could vary slightly from the plans used at the time of bidding. Unit prices help address minor differences between the actual site conditions and the plans, based on the limitations of existing surveys.

Consumer price index (CPI)-adjusted prices and lump-sum prices might be used by contractors or consultants, yet not enough information is provided to know about the use of either for a bid, to control variable quantities, and so on. A force account is a type of purchasing method for supplies or materials used that would apply to contractors doing work, not necessarily for variable quantities.

The answer is (B).

31. In 1994, the U.S. Secretary of Defense announced that the Department of Defense (DoD) would move away from military-unique specifications (MIL SPECs) and instead adopt industry standards. The objective of using performance and commercial specifications and standards is to enable the DoD to meet military, economic, and policy objectives. MIL SPEC reform is transforming the way the DoD provides and requires specifications. Federal, state, and local governments and agencies have formally adopted thousands of voluntary standards established by the American National Standards Institute (ANSI), and the process appears to be accelerating. For example, the Occupational Safety and Health Administration (OSHA) works closely with ANSI and its accredited standards developers, referencing over 200 of the 800 existing ANSI specifications for safety and health.

MIL SPECs are the general subject of the problem statement, yet that term alone does not address the change aspect of the problem statement. "DEFCON" is a military term that stands for "defense conditions" and refers to a defined set of alert levels that characterize states of defense readiness and preparedness. The term "homeland security" is broadly defined as a national strategy to make the United States safe from terrorist threats or attacks and includes activities related to federal, state, and local government—not just military sites.

The answer is (B).

Construction Administration

32. An administrative agency action will be made in this case because state boards are administrative agencies—part of the legislative, judicial, or executive branches. Landscape architecture practice violations are rare, and enforcement actions are even rarer, due to the many steps taken before a professional is licensed.

The remaining options are incorrect because each includes one of the three government branches yet does not include the administrative branch. A state board's budgets or appointments might be overseen by the governor (executive) or legislature, yet the board would be considered ministerial, regardless of how well funded or established it was.

The answer is (A).

33. Administrative practice is the type of professional assistance needed to respond to such an action by a state board. Each state has its own adopted administrative rules, and there is also a set of generally applicable national administrative rules.

A trial lawyer could not be used, because a state board hearing is not a judicial process. Malpractice might be a finding made by the board for license nonrenewal, but this response is incorrect because the problem statement does not specify that erroneous practice was at issue. Although "professional regulation" describes the general nature of the issue, this term does not clearly include administrative practice rules as a legal specialty service that a landscape architect might need to seek out.

The answer is (A).

34. Malfeasance refers to an erroneous professional action taken by a public official.

Misfeasance is a term related to a contract or a private action, not to public works. Although the term "malpractice" refers to the specific type of finding made by a board or a court, this response is incorrect because the problem statement does not indicate that practice was at issue in the complaint. Negligence means that a duty to act was not performed or an omission of some type was made, yet this term does not necessarily apply to an action of a public sector employee, as the term malfeasance does.

The answer is (B).

35. Clustering and transfer of development rights are both actions that may be taken to rearrange residential development for the protection of natural features. Clustering concentrates development in one area while avoiding another area. Transfer of development rights is a program or an agreement for relocation of residential density, possibly including the right to transfer development offsite to another property.

Capital improvement projects and periodic review of the adopted open space plan may help to preserve open space, but the problem statement does not provide sufficient information to warrant this assumption.

The answer is (C).

36. Buffers within upland areas may be used to reduce impacts to the edge of a wetland on a site with proposed residential development. Buffers can mitigate a wide variety of potential wetland impacts, such as sediment laden runoff that affects water quality or quantity, water level fluctuation from changes in runoff, wildlife predation or disturbance from domestic pets, and construction equipment damaging vegetation or compacting soils.

Water monitoring is incorrect because the problem statement specifies that only the wetland edge is at issue, and no information about amount or quality of water is given in the problem statement. The term "right of way" refers to a method of controlling ownership of a particular type of site development, yet the problem statement does not specify that access or utilities are at issue. Restriction of air rights will not accomplish impact protection at the edge of a wetland.

The answer is (A).

37. Abatement is the action that would be taken against a property owner to enforce code compliance. It authorizes removal of an improvement not allowed by code. In some cases, abatement costs are eventually paid by the property owner after a lien is filed on the property records.

Negation refers to repudiation, or canceling a prior action. An assignment refers to transfer of an obligation or contract from one person or firm to another. The term "addendum" is used for a directive to change an agreement.

The answer is (B).

38. Guaranteed maximum upset, billed hourly, is the form of fee arrangement used to ensure a client that the scope of a project will be billed at the actual number of hours, up to a maximum limit that the consultant will guarantee not to exceed.

Percentage of construction cost is a method of fee arrangement based on a portion of the project costs set by an estimate or actual bids. Percentage of prime consultant fee is a method based on a portion of the project costs, set using the prime consultant's fee amount in some percentage as the subconsultant fee. Yet this method does not ensure that the scope requirement will be met for any maximum fee. Cost plus fixed fee is similar to options (A) and (B), yet this method uses consultant's actual costs plus a negotiated lump-sum fee. While the cost plus fixed fee method does limit some expenses (the fixed fee portion) to a client, it does not limit the overall cost of services delivered to the client.

The answer is (D).

39. Assignment with right of survivorship is not a financial guarantee; it is a contract term related to contract survivability, or a contract's ability to remain in force after one main party is no longer available or eligible to perform. This contract provision extends the life of a contract agreement beyond one or more of the original contract parties, to an heir or successor. The problem statement does not indicate whether the assignment with right of survivorship has monetary value; it might only be the extension of an obligation to act or to refrain from action.

The remaining options are all types of financial guarantees routinely available from banks and insurance companies. They are used in the private and public sector to ensure that work can be performed by the contracting parties under an agreement, for the amount that is estimated or set for the work.

The answer is (D).

40. An architectural/engineering/planning (A/E/P) firm consists of professional services consultants, including landscape architects. Consultant firms typically would not be expected to include contractors or builders.

The remaining options are all types of companies that typically employ contractors as well as landscape architects who perform professional design services. However, these firm types are not considered consultant firms.

The answer is (A).

41. Reasonable skill and care is defined as standard care customarily found in the profession.

The remaining options include standard terms often found in contracts, bid documents, or professional services agreements. Standard specifications include outline formats such as the CSI MasterFormat™. General conditions might include standard care or reasonable care clauses, yet this general category does not define the term "reasonable skill and care." Performance conditions define the intended outcome yet do not specify the details or process needed to deliver the requirements.

The answer is (A).

42. Filing a petition with the clerk of court is the first ministerial action to start a construction claim in a court system. There are many types of court systems—municipal, county, state, province, appeals, tribal, etc. In some states or provinces, steps may be required prior to filing a construction claim. To determine if the construction claim merits the time and expense of claim resolution in court, states with enacted liability reform measures typically require that the party seeking relief first obtain a certificate of merit prepared by another independent professional.

The answer is (D).

43. A short list is a document of qualified consultants or contractors, and is used in the process of awarding a contract for a project.

An electrical punchlist—the list of remaining incomplete or unsatisfactory work tasks in the electrical system, such as a short in the electrical system—would not be directly in a landscape architect's area of expertise. An abbreviated or expanded note sheet for bidding would be called a support sheet. Option (D), "a method to ensure equal treatment of all interested bidders," does not comprehensively capture the meaning of the term "short list;" the qualification process used with a short list provides fair and equal treatment to all parties, yet uses past experience in a particular area of expertise as a primary factor in the decision among the likely finalists.

The answer is (A).

44. A request for proposals (RFP) is a method of locating and evaluating one or more potential subconsultants, such as a soils engineer or irrigation designer, for a federal or private project.

A request for information (RFI) is an interrogatory method that can be established by the project manager, a client, or a consultant as a means of formally requesting information during a consultant selection process, during a project, or during construction. Although lists exist for both minority business enterprise (MBE) and women-owned business enterprise (WBE) firms, these two kinds of lists are used only where required by federal, state, or local regulations, and their use is not standard practice. The overall goal is to ensure that an equitable distribution of consultant work will be performed by all firms, including those determined to be disadvantaged.

The answer is (A).

45. The consultant and the owner are the parties involved in an agreement for professional services.

A tenant and property owner would use a lease agreement. A contractor and subcontractor, as well as an owner and contractor, would use construction agreements.

The answer is (C).

46. The total current value of the contract, V_{total}, is calculated by starting with the contract amount, A, and then adding the three change amounts, ΔA.

$$V_{total} = A + \Delta A$$
$$= \$2,000,000 + (\$50,000 + \$75,000 - \$25,000)$$
$$= \$2,100,000$$

Retainage, amount paid, and number of payments made have no effect on the current value of the contract.

The answer is (C).

47. Insurers issuing errors and omissions professional liability policies find that as much as 70% of all litigation against consultants comes from miscommunication between the consultant and client. The remaining 30% of litigation includes actions by contractors or third parties and consultants.

Neither technical errors nor negligence resulting from incorrect design solutions is a large source of construction litigation against professionals, primarily because the continuum of the licensure process prepares landscape architects to avoid these situations. Construction safety is normally not the landscape architect's responsibility at a jobsite, and claims are low in that area.

The answer is (C).

48. Consultant, owner, and contractor relations on construction projects are greatly improved by project documentation processes.

Relations between the prime consultant and subconsultant, and communications between the general contractor and subcontractor are also improved as a result of project documentation; however, relations between these parties are generally already well established prior to the start of a project. Profitability could go up or down, depending on which party (owner, consultant, contractor) is burdened with overall project documentation costs. Alternatively, absorbing documentation costs may be a preventative measure resulting in higher short-term costs yet higher long-term profits (contractor, consultant, or owner), but this assumption can not be made from the information provided in the problem statement.

The answer is (B).

49. Financial firms (e.g., banks, insurance companies) typically refer to the process of surety bond release as exoneration. A surety bond is a widely used form of financial guarantee made available by a financial firm. A performance bond is a type of surety bond that offers a financial guarantee, specifically to ensure performance of work.

When a landscape architect prepares to make a request for exoneration, the process is called substantial completion or final inspection. For this to take place, a project must be substantially complete, usually excluding minor punchlist items. A final inspection would normally be required before making a request to release the surety bond. Expiration is incorrect because an expired bond would normally trigger some other type of action (e.g., renewal or litigation) rather than release of the bond.

The answer is (D).

50. The term "bidder's instructions" refers to documents that are not part of the technical specifications yet are added to the front of the project manual, which includes the technical and general specifications. The time and place to submit a bid can be found in the bidder's instructions. Other items found in the bidder's instructions include the invitation to bid and the bid form.

The remaining options are incorrect because all three are part of the specifications rather than the bid instructions.

The answer is (B).

51. The supplementary conditions, or special conditions, are the part of the project manual (also called the contract documents) that modifies the general conditions.

Although jobsite and weather information may be included in the special conditions, these factors alone are too narrow to define the special conditions. Special conditions do not normally modify technical specifications.

The answer is (C).

52. Clients are the largest single category of litigation claimants. Organizations that insure landscape architects report that 70% of all claims against consultants, including landscape architects, are filed by clients. One reason is that consultant firms tend to stay in business longer than contractor firms (9+ years for consultants versus less than 5 years for contractors). An additional reason is that, under state laws, the statutory time limits allowed for bringing claims against design professionals are typically longer, at 6 years to 10 years, compared to the time period when design-related claims are typically filed (more than 5 years after construction ends).

Subconsultants and general contractors are not the largest groups of litigation claimants against design professionals. Although third parties may be the largest type of claimants within specific categories of projects—such as public works and condominiums—they do not file as many claims as clients do, overall.

The answer is (A).

53. The general term "mechanics lien" includes materials liens, contractor liens, and consultant liens. In some states, the older term has been converted to "construction lien" to include all of the categories that supply labor, materials, or services.

Lis pendens is a legal term that means notice of pending litigation. Abatement refers to removal of an improvement or condition not allowed by code. A request for proposals does not refer to construction payment responsibility regulations.

The answer is (B).

54. Option (B) includes three objective factors—standards of practice, licenses held, and promotional materials—used in court decisions. This is verified by the experience of insurers, who see what courts actually use to make decisions in claims against professionals.

The remaining options may be found in courtrooms as asserted in claims involving a landscape architect. However, hearsay is third-party information and is normally limited by rules of evidence, public opinion is excluded or might be relevant only in limited situations, and anecdotal statements are less important than expert witness testimony.

The answer is (B).

55. The maximum time limit to pay a claim (civil) or provide punishment (criminal) is the statute of limitations, and this term can be included in specifications or in an agreement to control the potential for financial claims against a landscape architect consultant due to an error on the construction plans.

Statutes of repose describes the set of laws used to define the maximum time period for filing claims against professionals. These are not necessarily a limit on the number or type of claims, just a limit on the time period within which to file a claim. Indemnification is typically not addressed within the specifications, yet it can be part of an agreement or a part of the general conditions. Generally, a design consultant would not be able to obtain indemnification from a contractor; yet the professional could obtain indemnification from the owner, since the agreement for services would be with the owner, not with the contractor. The angle of repose is the maximum incline at which soil will remain in a stable position.

The answer is (A).

56. Three reasonable and proven contract clauses for condominium project liability control are 1) claim mediation, which is less expensive than litigation, 2) the client's agreement to waive claims up to a limit, such as the fee earned, and 3) indemnification, which limits third-party claims.

Bidding may help the project sponsor but not the consultant. Contractor safety is not an area in which landscape architects typically advise contractors. Certification by the landscape architect is risky since there could be recourse against the landscape architect for making statements based on incomplete or inadequate information.

The answer is (D).

57. The CPSC, or Consumer Product Safety Commission, is required by the Consumer Product Safety Act to rely specifically upon voluntary consensus for its consumer product safety standards, rather than to promulgate its own standards. The relevant portion of the federal law is as follows: "The Commission shall rely upon voluntary consumer product safety standards rather than promulgate a consumer product safety standard prescribing requirements described in Subsection (a) whenever compliance with such voluntary standards would eliminate or adequately reduce the risk of injury addressed and it is likely that there will be substantial compliance with such voluntary standards." (Source: Section 7(b)(1) of the Consumer Product Safety Act (15 USC 2056; PL 92-573; 86 Stat. 1207, Oct. 27, 1972, as amended in 1981.)) The CPSC topics most frequently related to a landscape architect's specifications are play structures and play-area surfacing.

The Construction Specifications Institute (CSI) is a nonprofit industry association that promulgates the most widely used specification referencing system. The American Wood Preservers' Association (AWPA) is the nonprofit organization that has been responsible for promulgating voluntary wood preservation standards since the year 1904. The American Water Works Association (AWWA) is an international nonprofit scientific and educational society dedicated to the improvement of drinking water quality and supply. All abbreviations listed might be found in a landscape architects' specifications.

The answer is (B).

58. The correct approach is to specify exactly which parts of the regulations the contractor must address during construction, for the scope of the project, and how this will be accomplished.

"Environmental regulations" is a broad term and could include those regulations that are beyond the control of either the landscape architect or contractor, such as equipment emissions and operations (clean air). The equipment manufacturer is usually responsible for meeting such requirements. Typically, the landscape architect writing specifications for the contractor is limited to requiring that the contractor "maintain all equipment to meet applicable OSHA and EPA emissions requirements."

Other areas of environmental regulation where both the landscape architect and the contractor typically have more control within construction specifications include temporary and permanent measures for sediment and erosion control (clean water) and wetland or stream protection (wildlife habitat).

Federal, state, and local environmental laws are typically quite extensive and are beyond the capabilities of the landscape architect to list or include in the specifications, or for the contractor to know. Excluding all responsibility might be an option for certain projects (e.g., a large corporation with its own environmental compliance staff providing this service), although not enough information is given in the problem statement to justify making this selection.

The answer is (C).

59. The component of the contract documents with more detail and specificity generally governs in the event of a conflict. Therefore, for private-sector construction specifications prevail over drawings. In federally funded projects, the drawings prevail.

For private-sector construction specifications are not equal to drawings, and drawings are not more important than specifications. Although codes do apply to construction contracts, the problem statement does not indicate that the matter of conflict between drawings and specifications is governed by code in this case.

The answer is (B).

60. The standards established by the American Society for Testing and Materials (ASTM) are widely used to define attributes for construction materials and are the standards primarily used in specifications.

The answer is (B).

61. A design/build firm is a professional business established to deliver both design and construction services. Each state has its own adopted administrative rules regulating design/build firms.

An architectural/engineering/planning (A/E/P) firm consists of architects, engineers, and planners; it represents one type of multidisciplinary firm. The problem statement does not define the type and range of professionals in the firm; therefore, multidisciplinary firm would be an incorrect choice. A limited liability company (LLC) might offer design and construction services, but this business format is not specific enough to properly address the question.

The answer is (C).

62. Either a modification to contract documents or a change order may be used to modify drawings or specifications.

A stop work order generally addresses the status of the work or schedule, not the contract documents. None of the remaining options would change the contract documents.

The answer is (A).

63. The shop drawings process addresses the need for more detail from a fabricator or supplier than the specifications or the drawings can provide. Landscape architects may be the review and approval authority of the shop drawings if they are referenced in the general conditions.

None of the remaining options—contingency; furniture, fixtures, and equipment (FF&E); and supplementary conditions—would add detail to specifications or drawings, yet all might be mentioned or included in the general conditions.

The answer is (C).

64. The need to establish a purchase amount for miscellaneous items that cannot be specified during the bid stage can be addressed by including provisions for a force account or cash allowance in the contract documents.

Cash subsidy implies a shared payment, not a method for purchasing items that might be difficult to specify. Reimbursement addresses which party might pay for an item to be purchased. A cash deposit may be used in lieu of a surety bond to ensure performance. None of the three terms specifically address specialized items purchased during the bid phase.

The answer is (C).

65. The errors and omissions coverage clause addresses risk and responsibility for the consultant, not for the contractor.

Explosion, collapse, and underground (XCU) and commercial general liability are insurance coverage types typically issued to contractors. Commercial general liability coverage applies to any type of firm and would also apply to contractors. Industrial insurance normally relates to manufacturing settings and locations, although contractors are covered under industrial insurance in certain states for workers' compensation, disability, or accidental injury in hazardous settings.

The answer is (C).

66. Incentive clauses and liquidated damages clauses address contractor rewards for early completion and penalties for late completion, respectively, primarily for schedule control.

Options (B) and (C) are conditions typically issued to contractors, yet not enough detail is provided in the problem statement to justify selecting these options. Commercial general liability coverage applies to any type of firm and would also apply to contractors. The force majuere and acts of war or terrorism clauses allocate responsibility or place limits on contracting party responsibility if major factors are beyond the contractor's control.

Two examples of work interruptions beyond a contractor's control would be the 2001 terrorism attacks in New York City and Washington, D.C., and the Fall 2004 category 4 Hurricane Katrina. The major-event hurricane damaged numerous properties located within a land area of 93,000 square miles. The hurricane materially changed the conditions of this land. Work contracted based on previous land assumptions could not be performed as contracted.

The answer is (A).

67. All answers seem reasonable, although the problem statement is primarily aimed at document control based on licensure. Option (B), sign and seal personal work, is the activity that is most central to licensure.

Following applicable laws is a licensure requirement, yet not enough information is provided to know about the software license, if any software was required to produce the drawing or report in question. Coordinating subconsultants' efforts is good policy, but the problem statement does not indicate that any subconsultants have been used in this case or that the landscape architect has this responsibility for coordination. Registering drawings with the patent office is also a good policy, yet the problem statement does not provide information about eligibility for copyright protection, whether the consultant has agreed to grant all copyrights to his or her client, and so on.

The answer is (B).

68. Probable cost of construction is the only type of construction cost estimate listed among the options. The remaining options are types of fee arrangements for consultant payment by the owner.

The answer is (A).

Assessment and Review

69. An easement is a defined portion of a lot, tract, or parcel reserved for use by someone other than the property owner. Uses can include access, utilities, or parking by another party who holds the easement interest or easement rights.

Private property could feature a dedicated public right of way, yet the dedicated portion in which the pipe was located would be public property, not private. And a dedicated city right of way would be public, not private. A restricted covenant describes or refers to site features but does not address ownership of a stormwater pipe. The term "lien" refers to a claim on an entire site or a portion of the site.

The answer is (A).

70. Because all U.S. cities (except for Washington, D.C.) are controlled by state constitutions, police power enabled by a state's constitution is the correct choice.

The remaining options are incorrect because, although the federal constitution and federal and state constitutional amendments may have some applicable authority, none of the three options includes basic police power held by the states, which the courts have determined is the source of municipal zoning power.

The answer is (B).

71. Common law must first be consulted as the proper authority to establish tree ownership. Next, the proper city code should be applied to determine what action to take.

The remaining options describe proper actions the owners might take after the tree ownership question is addressed, yet none of the three choices address tree ownership.

The answer is (A).

72. Because each state regulates the landscape architecture profession within its own jurisdiction, requesting reciprocity of the state in which the property is located is the correct choice.

Although a reciprocity process might not be offered in every state, responses (A) and (C) are incorrect because neither obtaining a CLARB membership nor relocating to the new state can yield registration in any state. Membership in a professional organization does not provide a license to practice in any state, so response (D) is incorrect.

The answer is (B).

73. A deed of trust is a legal document pertaining to property ownership and is required for real estate rights to transfer from one owner to another.

A survey of record might accompany a deed of trust as an attachment but will not yield a transfer of real estate when taken alone. A conveyance survey is the legal action (not a document) that clarifies property ownership. Although a quit claim deed can transfer real estate, more precisely, it is used to simply verify that any property ownership interest owed is relinquished by the quit claim deed document.

The answer is (A).

74. Sunset law reviews are conducted when legislation requires a periodic review to prevent automatic expiration.

Although it is a similar sounding term to the correct answer, sunrise law reviews is incorrect. Sunrise law reviews are found in the state of Colorado and refer to a mandated legislative review held to consider regulating a profession that is currently not regulated. Sunshine acts or laws, found in Florida, require public meetings to be open (rather than closed door) sessions. Recalls and referendums reject an elected person or existing law, respectively.

The answer is (B).

75. Through the licensure process, a practice act protects public health, safety, and welfare.

Property rights loss prevention is incorrect, since it is not specifically limited to landscape architecture. The public trust refers to some general right of the public at large, such as the right to shoreline access in coastal states. Alternately, public trust could be understood to refer to the intangible sense of confidence that a consumer or citizen might feel about the result of delivered professional services, although this understanding of the term is technically incorrect. Although it is true that the landscape architect derives a right to practice from a practice act, the main reason for a practice act is public health, safety, and welfare protection.

The answer is (D).

76. A title act, as differentiated from a practice act, protects the right to use the title "landscape architect" yet does not protect the right of a person or firm to engage in practice activity.

The protection of property rights or of public health, safety, and welfare might be reasons to have a title act, but the problem statement asks what these acts seek to protect. Public trust doctrine is a term that applies to general public-interest ownership and is unrelated to a landscape architect title.

The answer is (C).

77. CLARB's primary goal is to represent state licensing boards, as well as licensed landscape architects, nationally. Organizations are difficult to characterize, since they are often associated with many provided or perceived services. The response to this question is taken from a 1999 document entitled *LARE: A Guide for Professional Development*, edited by Virginia L. Russell, which the ASLA uses in the test preparation course offered at ASLA national conferences. The book is intended to guide those assisting LARE candidates with the test preparation process.

Dispute resolution is not a service provided by CLARB. Relocation assistance may be provided, but CLARB will not physically relocate a professional. Although there are close ties between the ASLA and CLARB, the main goal of the ASLA is to serve members who represent the profession on many matters, including licensure.

The answer is (B).

78. The term "zoning" is typically found only at the local level—in a city, county, or parish—and is, therefore, the best choice.

Aesthetic design control could be a local, state, or federal government function. Examples include a design board in a city, a state colleges design board, or a monuments commission for federal memorial sites or national monuments. Transfer of development rights and river basin management could also take place at the local, state, or federal level.

The answer is (B).

79. The term "watershed sub-basin management" might originate in federal or state law, yet refers to an activity that implies regional scale. Staffing for such a program is typically found at the level above an individual city or county, perhaps within a region of a state or within a region of several states. A few larger river sub basins might extend beyond state boundaries, yet the term "sub basin" implies that a state could define a portion of an entire river basin. Two examples of states with adopted and staffed regional watershed sub-basin programs are Washington (watershed resource inventory areas for hydropower and salmon protection) and Florida (watershed management districts).

An examinee might know and consider a few other exceptions that could make this question difficult to answer. In Hawaii, each major island (with several rivers) is a county, while Washington state has one county with several islands (and rivers). Thinking through the entire range, most would consider sub-basin management as a regional issue, whether the river is part of a county or several counties, part of a single state or several states, or extends into an adjacent country (Canada, for example).

Aesthetic design control is a local, state, or federal government level program, so it is incorrect. Examples include a design board in a city, a state colleges design board, or a monuments commissions for federal memorial sites or national monuments. Transfer of development rights is carried out at the local, state, or federal level. Zoning is a local (city or county) function.

The answer is (C).

80. Coastal zone management is based on federal law. It is typically administered at the state level and is not found at the local level.

Aesthetic design control is a local, state, or federal government function. Examples include a design board in a city, a state colleges design board, or a monuments commission for federal memorial sites or national monuments. Transfer of development rights is carried out at the local, state, or federal level. Zoning is a local (city or county) function.

The answer is (C).

81. The Federal Water Pollution Act of 1972 (Clean Water Act) implements the component program, the National Pollutant Discharge Elimination System (NPDES), through the work of civil engineers and landscape architects via temporary erosion and sediment control measures.

The Safe Drinking Water Act of 1974 and the Marine Protection, Research and Sanctuaries Act of 1972 are both incorrect because, although these programs relate to regulation of water quality, neither includes the NDPES program. The term "pollution," combined with the terms "erosion and sedimentation" in the problem statement, is the key to making the correct choice. The Resource Conservation and Recovery Act of 1976 is incorrect because it addresses pollution clean-up responsibilities of a land area for the site subsurface hydrology and does not include NDPES or temporary erosion as its main focus.

The answer is (C).

82. Zoning regulations typically define the floor area ratio (FAR) as the area of all floors of all buildings compared to the total site area.

On the LARE, the basic definition of FAR and use of the term "floor area" should be familiar to those practicing in most geographic regions. For test candidates with practical knowledge of adopted local zoning codes, the term "floor area" could potentially be confusing. Some jurisdictions (e.g., Canadian provinces) will use "gross floor area" to define "all floor area within buildings." Other jurisdictions (e.g., New York City) will exclude certain defined utilitarian interior floor area (e.g., mechanical rooms) from "gross floor area" when measuring "all floor area within buildings."

The FAR concept does not include either the ratio of the first-floor (or ground-level) footprint compared to the total site area, or the ratio of area of a site not covered by buildings compared to the area covered by buildings. The total number of floors compared to the site area is an indirect ratio similar to the FAR concept, but it does not directly relate the ground-level area or the area of all floors of all buildings to the site area.

The answer is (B).

83. The term "state" is present in two of the four possible options, allowing only (A) and (C) for final selection. Growth management includes regulation of population, density, traffic, and housing, as well as additional topics that affect the environment, therefore option (C) is the correct choice.

Regional regulations could be state, interstate, or intrastate in nature. When two or more states manage a single geographic area—for example, the Lake Tahoe region, or the Columbia River—it is typically known as regional planning, and such regions are created by federal regulations. "Environmental regulations" is too limiting as a definition of the term "growth management," yet environmental regulations are usually one part of overall state growth management regulations, as adopted in the states of Washington, Oregon, and Florida, for example. All three states have separate state laws for environmental protection yet also have environmental regulations within growth management regulations, so options (B) and (D) are incorrect.

The answer is (C).

84. Determine the correct choice by comparing the different uses of the term "critical" in all four options. Only option (B) differentiates the four responses with a key fact from the problem statement, because it includes the term "state." The term "areas of state critical concern" comes from the state of Florida's growth management laws.

"Critical lands" and "critical aquifer protection areas" are terms used in Washington state's Growth Management Act state law for two types of unique regions. Other growth management states—such as Hawaii, Vermont, California, and Michigan—feature similar terms, none of which is the generic overall category for all types of critical areas regulated by the state. "Critical unique environments" is a similar sounding term to the correct response but is not in customary use.

The answer is (B).

85. Codes, covenants, and restrictions (CC&Rs) are private regulations, or rules, that govern common-area structures managed by subdivision residents. Enforcement of the CC&Rs can be defined in the project administrative provisions within the CC&Rs. Typically CC&Rs are recorded at a public agency (state and/or local jurisdiction) so that access to the records is available to any party requesting action. Landscape architecture project administration includes advising a client how and when a set of CC&Rs might apply.

A homeowners association (HOA) and a limited liability company (LLC) are two types of legal entities that can be used to implement and enforce rules established by the CC&Rs. In most states or provinces, advising a client how and when to form an LLC and/or HOA would typically be the responsibility of a legal professional. An easement is an incorrect option because an easement can be used for structures that are public or private.

The answer is (C).

86. A setback is an area of a parcel of land located between the front, side, or rear of a property line and the buildable footprint limit area. There may be other types of setbacks, such a setback from the edge of a buffer, that may not necessarily be located at the front, side, or rear of a property.

Buffer and easement are incorrect because neither is exclusively located in a front, side, or rear yard. A set-aside program usually refers to a type of public-project contracting process or requirement for small or disadvantaged businesses, not to real estate.

The answer is (C).

87. Architects, engineers, and land surveyors are all state-licensed professionals, as are landscape architects.

Option (D) is incorrect because economists, who typically work with landscape architects for market research, are not licensed—although some states may register geologists. Option (C) is incorrect because the bar association, rather than state government boards, regulates and licenses attorneys. Option (A) is incorrect because, although sculptors and artists are highly valuable as frequent collaborators with landscape architects, they are not regulated at the state level.

The answer is (B).

88. The term "right of way" applies to the form of ownership of a street or road. In this situation, the street is classified as a proposed public right-of-way dedication because the dedication has not yet happened.

Even without knowing the definition of the term "right of way" or being familiar with the subdivision process, it is possible to choose the correct response by focusing on the time frames indicated by the four options. Focus on the adjectives "proposed," "recorded," and "dedicated" or "dedication" in the options, compared with the statement "in six months" in the problem statement, to determine that only option (B) could be correct. The proposed subdivision would have a proposed public right-of-way dedication if it were platted (recorded) in six months. Typically, the right of way formally becomes a right of way after it is platted.

The answer is (B).

89. The Army Corps of Engineers and the Fish and Wildlife Service are the largest U.S. agencies, in terms of staff and budgets, that have primary programs, published guidelines, and regulations dedicated to wetlands.

The remaining options are incorrect because the five listed agencies are proportionally less involved in wetlands regulation.

The answer is (A).

90. A landscape architect must not practice landscape architecture in a manner that violates federal or state law, and practice is not limited to related federal or state law. Some states have also identified specific laws that landscape architects must comply with as a prerequisite for first issuance of a license, such as payment of child support or repayment of student loans.

The damages mentioned in option (A) are not fully described, so it would be incorrect to assume that the landscape architect would be responsible for their costs under federal or state law. Option (B) incorrectly implies that it would be sufficient to practice under only those federal or state laws known to the landscape architect. In fact, it is the professional's duty to know which laws apply to his or her practice, and to comply with them all. Although minimum wage, immigration, and tax laws are not obviously related to landscape architecture, as real estate and environmental regulations are, compliance with these laws is required to practice once a license has been issued, so option (D) is also an incorrect statement.

The answer is (C).

References

Schatz, Alex P. *Regulation of Landscape Architecture and the Protection of Public Health, Safety, and Welfare.* American Society of Landscape Architects (ASLA).

Marshall, Lane. *Landscape Architect's Handbook of Professional Practice.* American Society of Landscape Architects (ASLA).

Your Complete Source for LARE Preparation
From Section A to E—PPI Has It Covered

Visit www.ppi2pass.com today!

─── **Comprehensive Review for Multiple-Choice Sections** ───

- Sharpen your problem-solving skills
- Assess your strengths and weaknesses
- Increase your solving speed and confidence
- Dual-dimensioned problems

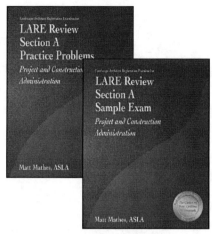

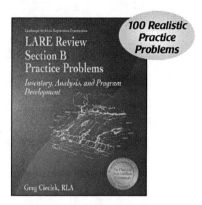

100 Realistic Practice Problems

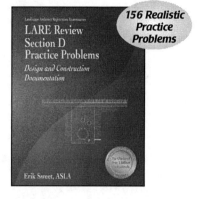

156 Realistic Practice Problems

LARE Review, Section A Practice Problems: Project and Construction Administration
Matt Mathes, ASLA

LARE Review, Section A Sample Exam: Project and Construction Administration
Matt Mathes, ASLA

LARE Review, Section B Practice Problems: Inventory, Analysis, and Program Development
Greg Cieciek, RLA

Topics Covered
- ✔ Analysis
- ✔ Inventory
- ✔ Problem Definition
- ✔ Programming

LARE Review, Section D Practice Problems: Design and Construction Documentation
Erik J. Sweet, ASLA

Topics Covered
- ✔ Construction Documentation
- ✔ Design Principles
- ✔ Graphic Communication
- ✔ Materials and Methods of Construction
- ✔ Resource Conservation and Management

─── **Practice Vignettes, Sample Exams, and Manuals for Graphic Sections** ───

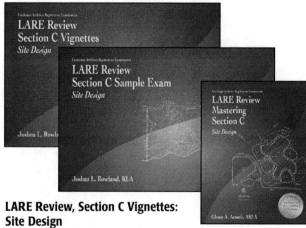

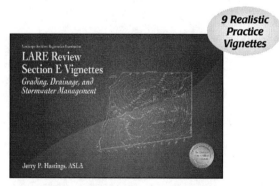

9 Realistic Practice Vignettes

LARE Review, Section C Vignettes: Site Design
Joshua L. Rowland, RLA

LARE Review, Section C Sample Exam: Site Design
Joshua L. Rowland, RLA

LARE Review, Mastering Section C: Site Design
Glenn A. Acomb, ASLA

LARE Review, Section E Vignettes: Grading, Drainage, and Stormwater Management
Jerry P. Hastings, ASLA

Topics Covered
- ✔ Grading and surface drainage
- ✔ Subsurface drainage

For the latest LARE news, exam advice, FAQs, and the unique community of the Exam Forum, go to **www.ppi2pass.com**.

Professional Publications, Inc.
www.ppi2pass.com